Amazing Animals

Tails

Measurement

Dona Herweck Rice

Whose tail is this?

A monkey's tail
is long.

Whose tail is this?

A pig's tail is short.

Whose tail is this?

A whale's tail
is heavy.

Whose tail is this?

A guppy's tail
is light.

Whose tail is this?

A beaver's tail
is wide.

Whose tail is this?

A mouse's tail
is narrow.

Which kind of tail is yours?

Is it long, heavy, or wide?

Problem Solving

Most dogs have tails. Some are long. Some are short. Draw pictures to show the lengths of the dogs' tails.

Bo

Fifi

Koko

1. Bo's tail is longer than a crayon.

2. Fifi's tail is shorter than a pencil.

3. Koko's tail is 3 erasers long.

Answer Key

1. Drawings should show tails longer than crayons.

2. Drawings should show tails shorter than pencils.

3. Drawings should show tails that are 3 erasers long.

Consultants

Nicole Belasco, M.Ed.
Kindergarten Teacher, Colonial School District

Colleen Pollitt, M.A.Ed.
Math Support Teacher, Howard County Public Schools

Publishing Credits

Rachelle Cracchiolo, M.S.Ed., *Publisher*
Conni Medina, M.A.Ed., *Managing Editor*
Dona Herweck Rice, *Series Developer*
Emily R. Smith, M.A.Ed., *Series Developer*
Diana Kenney, M.A.Ed., NBCT, *Content Director*
June Kikuchi, *Content Director*
Véronique Bos, *Creative Director*
Robin Erickson, *Art Director*
Stacy Monsman, M.A., and Karen Malaska, M.Ed., *Editors*
Michelle Jovin, M.A., *Associate Editor*
Fabiola Sepulveda, *Graphic Designer*

Image Credits: p.10 Stephen J Krasemann/Getty Images; all other images iStock and/or Shutterstock.

Library of Congress Cataloging-in-Publication Data

Names: Rice, Dona, author.
Title: Amazing animals : tails / Dona Herweck Rice.
Other titles: Tails
Description: Huntington Beach, CA : Teacher Created Materials, [2018] |
    Audience: K to grade 3.
Identifiers: LCCN 2017059896 (print) | LCCN 2018004937 (ebook) | ISBN
    9781480759572 (e-book) | ISBN 9781425856199 (pbk.)
Subjects: LCSH: Tail--Juvenile literature.
Classification: LCC QL950.6 (ebook) | LCC QL950.6 .R53 2018 (print) | DDC
    591.4/1--dc23
LC record available at https://lccn.loc.gov/2017059896

Teacher Created Materials

5301 Oceanus Drive
Huntington Beach, CA 92649-1030
www.tcmpub.com

ISBN 978-1-4258-5619-9